[ESSAY PRESS]

[I, AFTERLIFE] [ESSAY IN MOURNING TIME]

[KRISTIN PREVALLET]

[ESSAY PRESS]

I, Afterlife [ESSAY IN MOURNING TIME]

Essay Press is grateful to the College
of Arts and Sciences at Ohio University
and to a number of individual donors
for their generous support of this press.

Published by Essay Press
131 N. Congress Street
Athens, Ohio 45701
www.essaypress.org

Design and composition by Quemadura
Printed on acid-free, recycled paper
in the United States of America

ISBN-13: 978-0-9791189-1-3
ISBN-10: 0-9791189-1-3
LCCN: 2006939656

5   4   3   2   1

FIRST EDITION

[CONTENTS]

For Jane, David, and Elizabeth.

For grieving, everywhere.

*All of the author's proceeds
from this book will go towards
the Violence Policy Center's
efforts to treat gun violence
as a public health issue.*

[ALICE NOTLEY] [FROM "AT NIGHT THE STATES"]

At night the states
whoever you love that's who you
       love
the difference between chaos and
       star I believe and
in that difference they believed
       in some
funny way but that wasn't
       what I
I believed that out of this
       fatigue would be
born a light, what is fatigue
there is a man whose face
       changes continually
but I will never, something
       I will
never with regard to it or
       never regard
I will regard yours tomorrow
I will wear purple will I
and call my name

The narrative goes something like this:

My father walked into a hospital. Outpatient. He was suffering from severe panic attacks. He was sleeping two hours a night. He had to fill out a form: Name, address, birthdate. Is the patient suicidal? He checked "no." The next week, he drove to a gun store and bought a revolver. The next week, he drove to a parking lot and shot himself in the head.

Before this, he made an appointment to see a psychiatrist, and got a prescription for Paxil. The psychiatrist gave him a form: Name, address, birthdate. Are you suicidal? He checked "no." He only saw the doctor once.

There are numerous studies that link Paxil to suicide, but because he was depressed there is no reasonable proof that he was not suicidal before he took the Paxil. So this is a story that leaves a wide margin of doubt, a story that is not about probable cause.

On the day he died, November 20, 2000, it was overcast, but not too chilly. It's possible that he had tried to go to the gym at 5 A.M.

At some point, he bought *The Denver Post* because he used it to cover the windows of the car.

At 8 A.M. some kids from the neighborhood were on their way to the park. They saw the lone car in the parking lot, with the windows covered in newspaper. They peeked in and saw a man slumped over the steering wheel. One thought he saw blood on the man's ear. They called the police.

The police came to the house and asked, "had the victim been expressing suicidal thoughts?" They gave my stepmother a pamphlet, which included advice on how not to feel guilty. The pamphlet advised against building a shrine.

My stepmother wanted to see the body, to say a proper goodbye. The police told her to call the coroner's office. She called. They said, "You can't see the body. We'll leave his hand outside of the sheet for you."

We collected dried flowers from the garden and wrote letters so that my father would have something to open when he woke up on the other side. Zinnias, peonies, poppies, and strawberry bush brambles. We were trying to fill in the gap.

The report from the scene is the police-side of the story. 1) They searched for a pulse. 2) They established identity. 3) They took photos. 4) They wrote down descriptive phrases. (They investigated to make sure no foul play was involved.)

No evidence exists to call this "murder" because it cannot be proven that any outside force caused this violent act to occur. Internal violence is too intangible to be considered "proof."

So, as I was saying, after three days of being on Paxil, he drove eleven miles to Rocky Mountain Guns & Ammo on Parker Road and purchased a Colt revolver for $357. I asked my sister, "Who was driving? The man or the medicine?"

He signed a form: self protection. So, a man walks into a store and buys a gun for self protection. But self protection cannot protect the man from himself. I said to my brother, the logic escapes me.

The bumper sticker on his car read, "Conflict is inevitable, violence is not." The police didn't make a note of it on their report. The man who sold him the gun probably didn't notice.

The scene: a baseball field, in the heart of Englewood, Colorado. A field, and behind the field, a thick grove of trees concealing a bike path. One single and solitary tree sits off to the side of the field. A parking lot. He parked the car in the eighth spot, facing the solitary tree. When I went to investigate a few days later, I found a pile of glass. From this evidence I deduced his location at the time of death.

But this is not the whole story. The whole story is gaping with holes. The "hole" story is conflicted, abstract, difficult to explain.

Sublimation: when solid becomes ether without passing through the liquid state. When the overflow of negative psychic energy is rechanneled into writing, or art. When the distance between living and dying is filled in with language, objects, people, and mundane activities, such as doing the dishes. When something difficult to articulate finds its form in poetry. When death (silence) is brought back to life (mythology).

Regardless, the story has many possible forms and many angles of articulation. This is elegy.

[PART ONE] [FORMS OF ELEGY]

[MYTHOLOGY]

In time there are contraries and opposites.

In the sky there is either a savior or a flaming ball of fire.

The son and the sun are one and the same; they exist
    simultaneously but in different forms.

One and the other are one and the same.

Rocking forward and backward.

Wavering in the subatomic netherworld, preoccupied by thoughts
    of mourning.

[HOMONYM]

In the sun there is an I.

I am an organ that breathes, and through breathing come closer
 and closer to speech.

Eye is an organ that sees, and through the sea there is a passageway
 between fear, loathing, and anxiety; between vision and
 memory, and in reverse, between memory and desire.

Desire plays an important role in this essay.

She is not an angel but a double agent.

Double because she is yearning, and yet the very gaze she uses to
 seduce is the one that eventually will consume her.

The moth burns away, letter by letter:

Starting with "h," she ends up being just a word: *mot.*

The flame has made her French — her sign is on fire.

[DREAM]

I sat.

It was night.

Someone was in the room next door, waiting.

The noise was intolerable.

The unbelievable pulse.

The way of being with another while at war with the world.

The extension of it, the repetition.

The one and the other flowed.

Static, and then silent.

All the way down to becoming.

The means of arriving through and around the facts of longing,
and the need to extend beyond the personal and out towards
the intolerable present.

Through the words that are in me I tried to decipher the night,
and then remembered that darkness has its own resolution.

[DISTRACTION]

The lack is consumed with his thoughts.

I now believe that this world is nothing more than a means of
being in another.

There is the orchestra, the lawn, and the buzz.

The echo outside of my dreaming that occurs within me but is
actually only a projection. An antenna tuning in to the noises
of the forest.

Epictetus: play around with the power of moving towards an
object and retiring from it.

This gesture of approach is the closest you will get to the other
side.

[WILL]

That's me in a trance: solid, sound, and interrupted.

Over and over there are other stories, and other pauses that make
it difficult (if not impossible) to articulate the connection
between "loss" and "random objects."

One fills in for the other, although both remain empty and utterly
void of meaning.

I wonder how that can be, but then I remember my first attempt
to pour concrete into a body gaping with wounds.

I find this last sentence overly dramatic.

Please scratch it out.

[MARGINALIA]

Note the crossing-out of the text on the sheet of paper.

Note the markings of black that erase words and remove them
from view.

Note that because certain words are removed from view, certain
words therefore appear.

The words that appear to be important to you are the ones you
should follow.

Angles are sharp and a part of the line.

Don't turn corners too sharply or you might run over something
you once loved.

I remember when my father was happy, and I remember when
he began to disappear.

[ART]

A horsefly landed on my paper as I wrote this line.
I took a piece of tape and smothered it, pressing down on the
　　tape until the insect was flat.
Not finding it remarkable in and of itself (its wings are not
　　beautiful and its antennae are quite plain) I drew a rectangle
　　around the outline of tape.
The outline is supposed to resemble a grave, or a hole in the
　　poem where the insect can rest comfortably.
There is a connection between the insect and my father that
　　goes beyond the physical presence of one and the absence
　　of the other.
I know precisely what that connection is.
But you, in reading this, may never know.
I may refuse to reveal the truth of what I am mourning.

[DISTRACTION]

Grieving is tricky because suddenly a fly will appear and you
    will know right away that it symbolizes something much
    deeper than "fly."
Never believe maxims because all they do is comply with a
    sentence structure that is formulated in such a way as to come
    off as assured, wise, and mentally strong; they give those
    looking to fill empty spaces with words something to read.
Believing that holes can be filled with language is dangerous—
    only space itself occupies empty spaces.
So with this in mind, beware of being absorbed by an essay
    that is grieving, because you will lose your place and be
    eradicated, as quickly as the words on the page and as
    painfully as the fly.

[MAXIM]

Never fall in love with a text that attempts to convince you that
   you are already dead.
Or that says you are a vampire.
Or that makes you feel distant, aloof, removed from the scene.
Because the crime has already been committed.
You don't need to read about the gory details to know that it was
   violent.
We were both there, all along.
The only difference is that I see autumn leaves and immediately
   hear the gunshot.
You just want to see the body and marvel at how it fell forward,
   and then was left behind.

[FEAR]

Here is proof that one perception leads immediately to another:
  I have placed your heart on a platter to preserve it.
When you wake up you will find the bed already made and your
  chest neatly sewn.
There was never anything to fear except: who was the surgeon
  and did she sterilize her instruments?
Have I warned you not to fall in love with a girl who refuses to
  let go of grieving?

[GRAMMAR]

I am conscious that I am not using enough nouns in this text.

For example, car, stain, newspaper, and glass; notes, spruce,
and blood.

Steps that are horizontal and yet descend.

A chalked-off area in the parking lot.

A man who, working through something difficult, suspended his
fear of dying and shot himself in the face.

A man who, working through a knot, used a spinner to pry open
the tangle.

Maybe on the couch.

Maybe in an orchard.

Maybe on a baseball field.

Maybe as a way of finding perfection in a form.

A cold November morning. Silence.

[CONCLUSION]

This essay is not about nouns.

The clouds act like nouns.

A way of being in the present and noticing the rooftops, arrows,
    oceans, tundra, and possibly, the unified theory of everything.

Therefore, "nothing" is not a metaphysical question.

Just as "silence" is about all that cannot be spoken.

It is key to know that these words are written to dis-

APPEAR

The text that is grieving has no thesis: only speculations.

There is no resolution to this story because emotional closure is impossible.

"Nothing" is closure.

False closure: notes written at the scene of a suicide to express, narratively, the scene of the suicide.

Open closure: a sketch of black and gray space, a field upon which any act of violence can happen.

Scars, Marks, Tattoos: unknown.

Occupation: Retired.

Forced entry pronounced dead. . . . at 15:54 Hours. . . .

It had one spent shell in the cylinder (no other rounds in the gun).

They thought that seemed unusual.

I responded and took photos and evidence (after coroner arrived).

Fire/Rescue accessed the vehicle by breaking out the passenger door window with a spring-loaded punch.

I arrived ... I spoke ... he told me that the victim was
slumped forward ... a gunshot exit wound ... I asked ...
she arrived at the scene ... I was told ... I cleared the scene.

. . . unlocking of both of the vehicle's doors, the integrity of the scene was "not" compromised.

I was en route to the Sheriff's office in Littleton to end my
duty tour and responded to the area of the suspicious call
instead.

I noticed that the party inside was motionless . . . blood all
the way to his waist, saturating his shirt . . . the subject gave
all indications that they were deceased.

What is the language used to describe a person who has deceased?

Decease: it is the world that ceases existing, not the man.

Go away, depart, stop existing.

Except there was evidence. Something left behind. He was here.

When the sheriff came to pay his respects to our family, I noticed that he could not stop looking at my father's photograph on the wall.

Perhaps because he couldn't look at us.

Perhaps because he preferred this image of my father's face to the one he had encountered in the parking lot.

To the one that was left behind.

When a person has died the order of their things is weighed down by the fact that they will not be returning to move them. So the order of their things becomes a shrine; the order is preserved for as long as possible. Until it is clear that the person has actually left the room. I know this because the night after my father died I lay in bed half asleep and half awake. A panic began to overtake me, and I could not lie still. I clutched my head and walked into the dark living room: the panic was all around. The ceiling became shards of glass—they fell all around me. I lit a candle to calm the panic because it was as present as a person. I lay on the couch and stared at the candle. Beside me, his stack of books. He never stacked his books. They were always stacked as if he had been rumbling through, looking for something. He didn't seem to read books from cover to cover. On the top: *Manual of Zen Buddhism* by D. T. Suzuki. The book looked as if it had just been purchased from Barnes and Noble. He had stopped reading at page 30, *The Kwannon Sutra*. He scribbled the following notes on pages 14, 15, 16, 23, 26, and 29:

Vow to extinguish passion.
Perfect quietude—wisdom of absolute identity.
To keep one's thought pure.

(The birth + death of attachment. Blissful Tranquility beyond
*   birth + death).*
Nirvana is eternal, ever blessed, free from defilements.
Blessed One Enlightened One.
Self—nature is empty, Form is emptiness. We are not born,
*   we are not annihilated.*
Emptiness means the absolute or something transcendental.

We are not born. We are not annihilated. So where are we? Shards
of glass on the edge of breaking. On the verge of refracting a way
through, to another world. That this world be shard, the one beyond, smooth as glass. I never talked with my father about ghosts.
Except that once, we encountered one.

There is a story about an old man who encounters the ghost of who he wants to be; there is a story about a man and the mountains. Like any sea these mountains have a name, they are called "Rocky," and upon the crest of the range there is a trail that enables a person to walk across five states and through five separate ecological life zones.

There is also a story about a specific point on a specific trail. Follow the crest of the range. The thick groves of aspen and pine open onto a clearing. Much like being on a boat in the middle of a tumultuous sea, watching as the waves slowly calm. The moment when the world beyond the waves suddenly opens up to all of the possible worlds that are hiding within it. And things are finally clear: there is a place on earth where the sky and the mountain like the mountain and the sea are one and the same: the mountain piercing the watery sky and the sky flowing down over the mountain.

> *The clarity of the sky prevents its falling. The firmness of the earth prevents its splitting. The strength of the spirit prevents its being used up. The fullness of the valley prevents its running dry. The growth of ten thousand things prevents their dying out.*
> [TAO TE CHING]

One day, my father took me to a specific trail on the mountain and there we met an old man. His face was worn with tough wrinkles; he wore a hat that was tattered but functional; he was well-layered and his backpack was as big, and perhaps as heavy, as a deer.

He told us that he had been walking the trail since Montana, that he had been walking for three years, and during those years the only people he saw were the people he met on the trail.

We were amazed by this man, his endurance, his loneliness, his withdrawal from the world, his persistence in walking, the fact that through walking he had *become* the mountain, that indeed there was really no way to separate him from the mountain because it had made its impression on him.

He could have been the spirit of the mountain, he could have been a ghost, he could have been the breeze of the aspen as it brushed through the fur of a hare.

This old man made me see that my father was utterly disconnected from the ground he was walking on. I noticed how he was walking ahead of me with a pace not at all suited for the terrain. Unlike the old man, my father's questions—about the cosmos, space, time, the universe, the one God of the present and the many gods of ancient times, the galaxy and the peace of being in nothingness—were not rooted in his experience of walking, here and now, through the mountains. It seemed to me that these questions were in fact sending his mind into a spiral of confusion that gave him no insight into how to live a life worth leading.

I too am occupied by all the questions of my father, and like him I wonder if the void is too great, if time is too vast, if humanity is too imperfect; and like him I sometimes wonder if it all isn't remarkably futile, if enduring the persistance of fear and disappointment in our lives makes sense in the quest for an overall purpose.

This story, about a man who meets the ghost of who he wants to be, has already been told, over and over:

> the man has disappeared, no traces are left, the bright moonlight is empty and shadowless with all the ten thousand things growing on it, if anyone should ask the meaning of this, behold the lilies of the field and their fresh sweet-scent. [D. T. SUZUKI]

Take back the preparation
the flour from the bread
the citrus from the fruit
or the sweet, take it away
from the melon
make it rindy and hard
or the moisture from the clouds
make them lighter
and transparent
if the blue
was taken away
from the sky
everything would be black
the particles from the light
take them away
make the objects of the earth
disappear.

Give back the fruit
the flowers
they came so unexpectedly
why not give back the baskets
the cheese and all the meatloaf
and the car
it could be given back
to the driver
and pointed
in another direction
give back the pine trees
to the park
the parking lot to the birds
or the air to silence
give back the field
to the football players
all could begin again
as new it all could be given back
the glacier to the snow
give back the knee-deep tread
all of this
all these things could be
and then again
all over.

The glacier is not cold
is not a person snow
who decides to return to water?
The wind is not dry
is not a person winter
who decides there is no reason to fly?
The air is not liquid
is not a person ocean
who decides there is no reason to breathe?
If the light were to expose
itself as light
would there really be
any reason to see?

If beings are to be saved by his assuming a state-officer's form
the Bosatsu will manifest himself in the form of a state-officer
and preach him the Dharma. [THE KWANNON SUTRA]

If a person is to be saved by a herd of elk
then a herd of elk will appear to the person
and lead him to the sunward side of the mountain.

If a person is to be saved by a mountain lion
then a mountain lion will appear to the person
and lead him across the river.

If a person is to be saved by a bee
then a bee will appear to a person
and lead him through the sun.

If a person is to be saved by a person who understands the Dow
then a person who understands the Dow
will appear to the person and teach him about investments.

If a person is to be saved by a junkyard dog
then a junkyard dog will appear to a person
and lead him to the pot of gold.

If a person is to be saved by a pilot
then a pilot will appear to a person
and lead him through the rain.

If a person looking for an object is to be saved by a shopkeeper
then a shopkeeper will appear to a person
and lead him to a different object than the one he is looking for.

If a person is to be saved by a person driving a truck
then a person driving a truck will appear to the person
and push him off the road.

If a person is to be saved by a person opening a window
then a person opening a window will appear to the person
and lead him into the house.

If a person is to be saved by a person
helping another person to jump-start a car
then a person helping another person to jump-start a car
will appear to the person and lead him through the electric charge.

If a person is to be saved by a person
walking with another person who is looking at a plane
then a person walking with another person
who is looking at a plane
will appear to the person
and lead him into the future.

If a person is to be saved by a person
hitting another person who was the person being hit,
then the person hitting another person who was the person being hit
will appear to the person and lead him to the cave.

If these people and then these people appear to a person
then all these people are here to lead a person home.

If a person does not want to go home
then he will be led to the mountain
and there he will disappear.

If a person disappears on his way to the mountain
then another person will arrive at the mountain
and will know that the mountain has led this person into the glacier.

[PART TWO] [THE DISTANCE BETWEEN HERE&AFTER]

Elegy is anti-afterlife. Afterlife presents itself as an assurance of a habitable unknown, a space that exists in time where the person being mourned is no longer invisible because he has been reborn. The hopefulness of the afterlife is the despair of the present—there is no proof that life-after-death exists, and this makes the suffering inflicted by the present intolerable. Elegy, on the other hand, allows the difficulties associated with dealing with suffering—grief and loss—to be represented without closure. Afterlife is a tidy package that presents a simple truth. Elegy is the complexity of what is actually left behind.

When, suddenly, instead of the world revolving around a person, a person becomes aware that the world is chaotic and impermanent. Anyone she knows or anything she owns can disappear: the world's surface shimmers like a thin wall of water. The logical way to handle this is to intellectualize, rationalize, and anticipate the events of the world so that there are no surprises: to use language as if it can possibly steady what feels so tenuous and uncertain. But there is nothing certain about language, just as there is nothing certain about where a person goes after he has disappeared.

(this lack)

　　　resistance

no articulation of singular truth

　　　　scattering of language and forms

　(resist closure)

scratch at the surface of the lie:

　　　　there is a surface and an unknown

　　　　　　　　　　that is surfaceless.

Otherwise:

I fear that the sadness of the present will not be reconciled by
　　the future.

Restate:

There is an absence of any system that might transform the
　　sadness of the present into a hopeful future.

State again:

Where is the ideology, the paradigm, that will reverse the
　　sadness of the present?

Again:

Where are all the people going to go when the structures put
  into place to sustain them are dismantled?

Eddie Berrigan:

"They say that the meek will inherit the earth but who will
  inherit the meek?"

Or:

Who will the earth inherit?

The elegiac burden is the poem expressing, through the form it takes on the page, the broken minds which have shaped it. The poem is a state of both mind and landscape, and because it is not mappable, is capable of articulating a person's spatial distance. The poem, scratched out on the surface of the page, scratches then at the surface of the world "outside" of the poem. The success of this is articulating something difficult; perhaps even articulating something so well and so persuasively that readers are inspired to seek clarity in their relationship to loss, disappointment, or fear. The sadness of this is the difficulty of knowing that what the poem knows—or rather how it knows—will probably not change the world. And yet, people die every day from the lack of poetry in faith. In doubting the possibility of a tidy afterlife, I have come to compose a fragmented system of believing. I call this poetry.

Come back
to three lines of light on a little river—
one pink, one green and one aluminum—
come back to being.

[FANNY HOWE, "THE PASSION"]

What is the connection between "taking back" and "coming back?" Taking back means going back into time and shifting the course of events so that a painful moment (such as a person dying) will not happen. Coming back means daring to ask that the dead intersect with this time, the present. Both are impossible. But it is the desire for time to be interrupted—by either a going or a coming back—that is the elegiac burden. Poets enter this space with language. Language fills in the desire to alter time. This creates distance: using words even when it seems that there are no words that could possibly express the suffering associated with loss. Distance is not a means to "express" nor a means to "represent" what is missing—it's a way to fill in the space left when something that was once visible has disappeared and left a gap. What fills the gap: forms of elegy.

There are the states—Alabama, Alaska, Arizona, Arkansas—and there are states of mind. There is an immeasurable distance between the mind and geography that makes walking through a landscape tenuous. Your feet may be touching the ground, but where is your mind? The map that connects the land to the mind is not three dimensional, or even capable of representation. It is an unmappable cartography measured by space, gap, and distance. Certainly presence and awareness can connect a person to the land they are treading. But usually, a mindset of spatial distance prevents a person from ever being one with the world.

The lack of communication between the living and the dead makes the living wild with fear. It is in this distance, the space between, that grieving finds form in poetry. This form scatters its content into sometimes incommunicable terrain, diffusing meaning (splatter) as if trying to connect the multitude of suffering. Being open to receive this splatter of meaning hesitantly transmitted through difficult language is one way to practice living with uncertainty and doubt. Be. Negatively. Capable. Commence. Again. One more time. Start over. Here.

The steady shadow
among the many moving around it

is a priest handing out prayers wrapped in cakes
sneaking a blessing on any takers

even if there are none, and the crowd
keeps walking without noticing

their heads are bent, mourning
what they do not know

but it is this: that the other side
has met many unprepared

too exhausted with pain and the lack of language
to notice that something has entered

where before no one dared
to whisper: *commence.*

cruel

etc.

trappings

Oh! allow—no

you still want . . .

[STÉPHANE MALLARMÉ,
"A TOMB FOR ANATOLE"]

The poetry of my language is broken by the realization that it can do nothing more than fill in the division between silence and pain with arbitrary, black-and-white letters. If the body of the text has suffering at its root, then language will take a fragmented, torn-apart form, as if it too is suffering. Poetry that seeks this kind of engagement with language is positioned to absorb the brokenness of grief. And as the century's end and the century's beginning point towards the swift co-opting of humanity by a global economy that could care less for human needs outside the need to spend money, the elegiac tradition as it evolves is perhaps no longer concerned with articulating the unspeakable ::::::::::::::::

::

::

::::::::::::::

::

::

::

::::::::::::::

but rather with. . . .

rather. . . .

The sentence cannot be completed.

At least not how it began.

To start again.

Putting a form to something that is absent (i.e. writing a poem to stand in for the emptiness felt when someone close to you dies) happens in the social realm as well. There are monuments: forms that stand in for an absence, that attempt to seal the ground which, without a monument, would be impressionable space. The most successful monuments are the ones that allow the person reflecting to have his or her own experience. The monuments in public parks, those gigantic steel statues of men on horses, are too determined. But regardless, this tendency to put up monuments is a human fact, one that is ancient and harkens back to the functions of totems—to bridge the gap between the earth and the heavens. To bridge the gap, that is, between what is visible and invisible. The dead are invisible; they inhabit spatial distance. Think of the debate around the memorial that would be most fitting to the grief caused by the collapse of the World Trade Center. Is it a personal grief? Financial grief? International grief? National grief? Religious grief? How to memorialize an event that in its wake has left tens of thousands of people dead (Istanbul, Iraq, Afghanistan, New York, Lebanon, Palestine, Israel, Saudi Arabia and on and on and on)?

There is no photograph
that can allow those of us who have never experienced
it to have a memory of war.

Every image of "horror" becomes a loop.

He saw a movie every night
(of his actual experience)
in his mind

goat-women sliding down poles,
child alone in rubble
the surgeon
gone with his liver
broke the needle
straight into her eye.

The moment of fear
is the moment to attack

above, behind, within

bottle, shotgun, roadside bomb, missile

"the fear is all over your face"

Tell that to the giraffe
who falling down

followed her horn
to soften the blow.

Our eyes are not the only way we see things. Is this what
    I'm trying to say?

See the heron that whether flying

                         right-side up
                         or upside down
still looks the same.

See the paper floating high into the air
                         with the morning news
                   not weighing heavy enough
                         to tilt the election
          or bomb the house.

The bird refuses

to commit
               and remains
                   (upside or downside)

         unread, either way.

If you have memories of war from seeing photographs of dead bodies stacked one upon the other in mass graves; if you have memories of war from seeing movies where shrapnel enters a body in slow motion and shreds it into chunks; if you have memories of war from reading the Iliad: "the point of bronze pierced the bone, and darkness veiled his eyes." Perhaps these images of war have allowed you to have memories of war even if you yourself have never actually been in a war. Some would say that graphic images of war, because they allow people to see to its horrors, might work to provoke anti-war sentiments. But no wars have been stopped by these images.

"How mighty are the fallen"
tree-necked and crashing

to the ground
sacred spotted giraffes

pistol-bound to the throat
two-directional hit

one up, one down
red is a fountain

gushing uncontained
twinned-horns

collapse standing
yet falter, falling

felled and left there
buzzard-beckoned

hailing "the end
of the world."

I'm a shrine builder. Many people who have experienced loss in their lives are—this loss isn't necessarily the death of a loved one, it could be a more interior loss, a sense of abandonment, a sense of betrayal, a fragility of no matter what kind. My tendency to shrine came about after my mother died in 1986. I started keeping objects in the corner of a room. Sometimes these objects meant something to me, sometimes they didn't. The objects in the shrine change every so often. At times, I'll create a special box for my shrines; at other times, I'll make a whole altar with incense, candles, and bowls. In a handout that the police gave my step-mother after my father's death, there was a section on shrine building which stated that in order to get through the twelve stages of grief with maximum efficiency, one should dismantle any shrines. As a political position, I hold on to grief. The objects in my shrine represent this. I don't see it so much as holding on to my dead parents, but rather as holding on to an awareness of spatial distance. The objects in the shrine keep my hold on reality consistently tenuous because they fill my gaps with objects that are constantly changing. (Which is better than filling spaces with a false sense of closure. There is no moving on in a world filled with wars.)

Here are some of the objects in my shrine.

(Which has no closure. Which is constantly being rearranged.)

A statue of a clown.

A rubber fish.

A few flat rocks.

A doll.

A lone earring.

A medicine bottle from the 1940s.

Beads from several broken necklaces.

A batting glove.

A pen and pencil set marked with the words "Marcos" and "Ramona."

A Buddha head.

A deer vertebra.

A stack of postcards.

Two small urns filled with ashes.

A stack of pesos and francs.

The keychain I used to carry in high school.

A broken pewter statue of the grim reaper.

I'm filled with holes. I used to seek spackle in my relationships with people. And I still have a hard time holding on. But really, there is nothing to be filled in. Knowing this gives me some comfort because it means that I have to live with my losses as one would live without an arm: being constantly aware of the phantom limb sensation that wants so desperately to connect, to be filled in, with flesh. But ultimately, I have to survive by rewriting the script that assumes that spaces have to be filled in. They don't —like the universe, my holes are filled with their own energies, forces fields, and pulls. The challenge is to recognize this antimatter as some kind of sustenance; to find in holes a certain kind of completion.

The story of my first attempt to manifest spatial distance:

One day, after my mother died, I went fishing in the mountains with my father. He was ahead of me along the stream that ran through a flat field, yellow, it was fall, we had jackets. Being that I could see all around me, peripheral vision meant no ghosts could jump out at me. The fact that it was a field with no trees meant no one could retreat into hiding once they made themselves seen. In other words, I dared my mother's ghost to appear in what I deemed to be a safe space. I said, if there is an afterlife, then make a fish jump now. Nothing happened. I said, make a dragonfly appear across my line of vision now. Nothing happened. I said, make the clouds form any letter of your name. I strained to see the letter "A" in the sky, but could not beyond the shadow of a doubt see anything but clouds. The stream—nothing was more than what it was. Nor the insects, nothing more than what they are. I concluded that there is no afterlife. My father appeared with two fish, he put them in the cooler. I looked back at the stream as we drove away, but there was nothing. I saw what was there. Only this: it was autumn.

[ACKNOWLEDGMENTS]

This book is a revision and gathering together of poems and essays written from 2000 to 2006.

"Essay on the Sublimation of Dying" appeared in different form in *The Seneca Review* (vol. 35, no. 1). Thanks to Deborah Tall.

"Crime Scene Log" and "The Voice Variously Heard" appeared as an A.BACUS chapbook (no. 153). Thanks to Dan Featherston and Peter Ganick.

"The Voice Variously Heard" appeared in *Insurance* (no. 3). Thanks to Kostas Anagnopulos and Chris Tokar.

"The Old Man and the Mountain" was written as the eulogy for my father's funeral, St. Barnabus Church, Denver, Colorado, November 25, 2000.

"The Distance Between Here&After" was first written as a response for a forum on elegy in *LIT: New School Literary Journal* (no. 5). Thanks to Joy Jacobson for asking me to write this piece. It was later revised for a talk given in October, 2003 at The Poetry Project at Saint Mark's Church. Thanks to Prageeta Sharma. Six sections appear in my book *D'un devenir fantôme: Formes poétiques en temps de deuil* (cipM/Un Bureau sur L'Atlantique, 2006). Thanks to Juliette Valéry and Emmanuel Hocquard as well as co-translators Omar Berrada, David Lespiau, Pascal Poyet, and Sarah Riggs.

Thanks also to Alice Notley, Elizabeth Willis, Joan Retallack, Maggie Nelson, Eléni Sikelianos, and Akilah Oliver, the invisible and unacknowledged legislators of this manuscript's struggle to find language and form for hard-to-articulate mental and emotional spaces. Thanks to Catherine Taylor, Stephen Cope, Eula Biss, Richard Ryan, Elaine Prevallet, and Jeff Clark for their pivotal editorial suggestions and overall support for this project.

[ESSAY PRESS]

is dedicated to publishing innovative, explorative, and culturally relevant essays in book form. We welcome your support through the purchase of our books and through donations directly to the press. Please contact us to be added to our mailing list.

EDITORS: Eula Biss, Stephen Cope, and Catherine Taylor

ESSAY PRESS
131 North Congress Street
Athens, Ohio 45701

www.essaypress.org

New and forthcoming titles from Essay Press:

The Body: An Essay JENNY BOULLY
Letters from Abu Ghraib JOSHUA CASTEEL
Griffin ALBERT GOLDBARTH
Adorno's Noise CARLA HARRYMAN